ACTUAL... INTO CONCRETE TERMS YOUR THOUGHTS

HUMAN
HIDE UNDER MATTER ANIMATED IN THE NOW

LIFE MINISTERING TO LIFE ITSELF

WHY YOU DO

LIFE AFTER LIFE ?

WHAT YOU DO

BY THINKING OF THE END RESULT AS IF IT HAS ARRIVED

An
Adventurer's Guide
to the Jungles
of Time and Space

TUT
DOT
COM

Copyright ©2012 by Mike Dooley
Adapted from Mike Dooley's Lost in Space, © 1998 TUT Enterprises, Inc.

Published by Totally Unique Thoughts®
A Division of TUT® Enterprises, Inc.
Orlando, Florida · http://www.tut.com

Printed on acid-free paper. Vivella® book cover from Italy.
Manufactured in China.
Design & Illustrations ©2012: Susan Gross, www.susangross.com
with Lisa H. Soltes, www.ten2ocreative.com
Edited, Copyedited by Hope Koppelman

Library of Congress Control Number: 2011941619
ISBN: 978-0-9814602-5-3
ISBN: 978-0-9814602-6-0 (ebook)

YOUR NAME

was whispered

before you were born,

and as if from the mist

your image took form.

The Spirit of Life

had begun its quest,

to learn of itself

through the ultimate test:

A Being of Light

set free in creation,

to master the gift

of imagination.

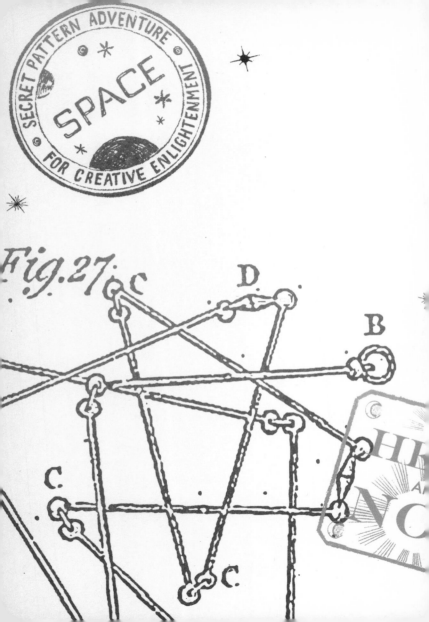

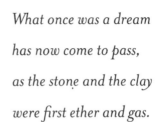

What once was a dream
has now come to pass,
as the stone and the clay
were first ether and gas.

CHAPTER

1

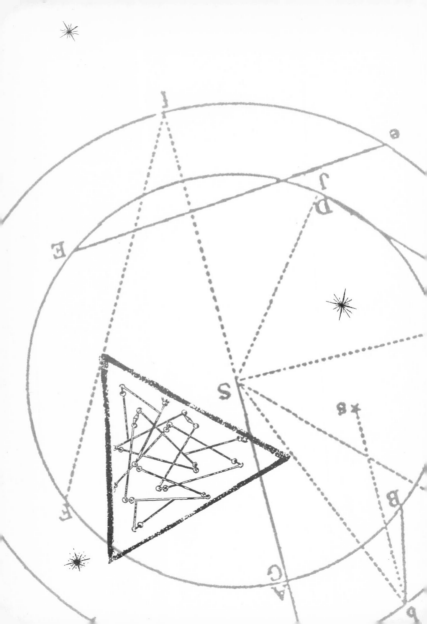

Not all that long ago, in the nether reaches of ad infinitum, there formed a council of fearless explorers — Adventurers much like you — who had become bored with perfection, infinity, and all the trappings so familiar to those who art in heaven. Whatever it was they wanted, they got. However they wanted to change it, they did. And whatever they wanted to be, they became. Their existence had become so "same old, same old" that they hardly felt like the great Adventurers they were. It wasn't enough, they agreed; something had to be done.

So, being who they were, they decided to invent an entirely new dimension for their reality.

Well, new dimensions, even for these Adventurers, don't get invented all that often, so you can imagine their excitement as they began to explore the vast new possibilities that suddenly lay before them. And this dimension was especially cool because it made possible the previously unthinkable ability of being in just one place, without being everywhere else at once.

Of course they were really still everywhere else at once, because back then in the nether reaches of ad infinitum

there was only the here and now;

nothing else existed. Which meant these

poor explorers never had anywhere to go

because they were already everywhere! Yet

because of this new dimension, they were

now actually able to dim their awareness

of everywhere else

enough to

focus on

being a single

"somewhere" at a

time. Obviously, however, more

than inventing "somewheres,"

what they were really learning to do,

A GREAT OMNISCIENT GOD DEITY

11

momentarily at least, was to blot-out everywhere else from their thinking, except for where they "thought" they were.

Now to you, this may all sound pretty tame, but to them it was revolutionary. You see, up until then, such separations from one another, here versus there, had been practically impossible because they had all simply been One, a Great Omniscient Deity, or GOD.

True... they *were* still God in this new dimension, because God can only be God, but it did allow them to have a totally unique perspective on their reality. For instance, each of them had a secret

pattern they could follow to orchestrate
their very own magic and experiments,
in virtual secrecy. And instead of just
being the cosmos in its entirety, now they
could actually travel through it, from one
somewhere to another. Imagine... after
eons and eons of just hanging out, now
they actually had *places* to go.

So much did they learn and refer to
this new dimension that it quickly became
known as the Secret Pattern Adventure
for Creative Enlightenment,
or SPACE for short.

BY THINKING OF THE END RESULT AS IF IT HAS **ARRIVED**

MATERIALIZE
ANY
THOUGHT
THAT
EXISTED
INTO
REALITY
MATTER

In the game of life
your dreams will come alive,
by thinking of the end result
as if it had arrived.

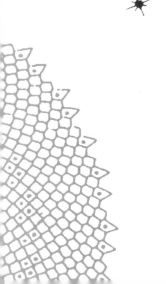

CHAPTER

2

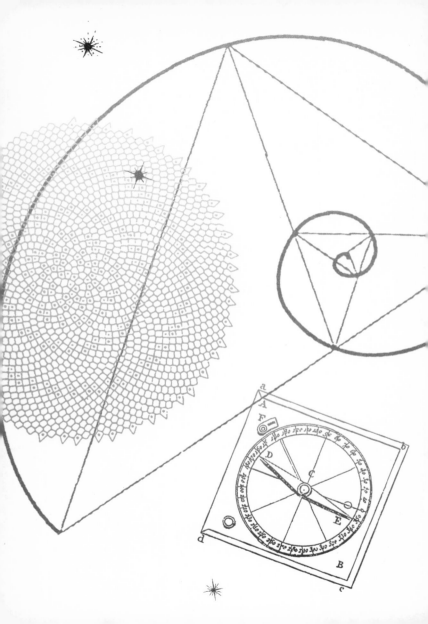

The Adventurers were on a roll, and inspired by their burning desires, it didn't take them long to realize that this SPACE of theirs contained far more possibilities for fun than even they had dreamed of. And best of all, they were beginning to see that this SPACE, itself, could be *filled*! With what? With the only thing that has ever existed, of course... thought!

They had long known of the absolutely awesome powers of thought, but they had never thought about what a thought, itself, might look like... or how it might sound, or how it would feel, or smell, or taste...

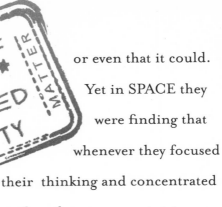

or even that it could.
Yet in SPACE they
were finding that
whenever they focused
their thinking and concentrated
their thoughts, the energy sent out was
actually transformed... with shocking and
spectacular results. Their thoughts, all
on their own, became dense and appeared
solid. Aghhh!! In other words, they seemed
to *come alive*!

In SPACE, the Adventurers were
finding that their thoughts could appear
big or small, green or red, hard or
soft, loud or quiet, *whatever* they

imagined. It was so easy, that it seemed too easy. But easy or not, it was quite apparent that their thoughts only needed to be "thought-of" to take form and be projected into this new dimension that held them.

Of course the Adventurers had used their imagination before, but now, in SPACE, a manifested thought could be examined from the outside-in, giving it a multidimensional reality all its own. And "things" really got rolling when, to their delight, they found they could Manifest Any Thought That Existed into Reality. So in no time at all

(mostly because time had not yet
been invented), MATTER began
to fill their SPACE.

Creativity soared amongst the
Gods as they dabbled in
first creating stars and
planets, and then
mountains and oceans.
Everything they dreamed
of came to life in an
explosion of light,
color, and sound
that stretched their
imagination to the very edges
of their SPACE. It was *fantastically*

exciting,

except...

except deep

down inside, they

knew that something was missing:

as spectacular as their new worlds were,

they themselves, the creators of

it all, remained on the

outside, looking in.

BY THINKING OF IT AS IF IT HAS ARRIVED THE END RESULT

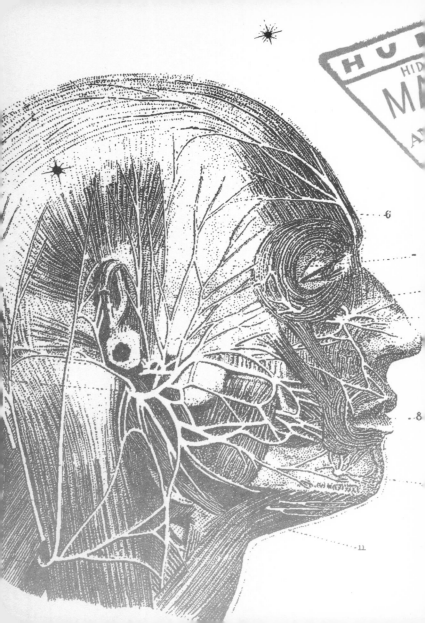

Time and space

aren't quite as they seem…

just magical props

in a magical dream.

So the Adventurers began to ponder how
they could become part of the mysterious,
enchanting, material worlds they had
created, and in their wondering they asked,
"If our MATTER is simply
occupied SPACE, and as God we
are really everywhere at once, hmmm...
could we possibly exist in the very same
SPACE that holds our MATTER?"

Immediately they knew that they could,
and as they thought it, they did it,

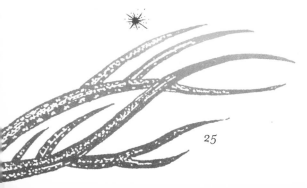

taking-up residence inside their MATTER,

just as if it were a somewhere (by

momentarily blotting-out everywhere

else from their thinking)!

Right about then, as if "things"

weren't interesting enough

already, a new game

was being invented

called "hide-and-seek,"

and as could be predicted,

the Adventurers scurried about

in their excitement and hid

themselves inside their creations where

they would not likely be found. They Hid

Under Matter Animated in the Now,

because "Now" was still all there was,

and when they referred to

themselves hiding, they

called it being

HUMAN.

It was a great idea,

this hiding under

MATTER, so great in fact,

that no one was ever found! So

despite their joy in having found a new

game to play, they were no longer aware

of each other's discoveries. Big problem.

This prompted a call to go out for the

need to Trace

one another

In Material Existence;

thus TIME was born, finally!).

The games resumed, reunions were planned, and the fun really began—until, that is, everyone had pretty much "Been there, done that!" as they liked to say.

Another idea was needed, and still as God, because God can only be God, it didn't take them long to have one. What if, they thought, we all ventured out together, HUMAN, into the *same* SPACE, at the *same*

TIME? WHOA!
This idea was so
monumental, so
profound, so colossal…
that it sent a big bang
booming throughout
all creation, and has since been compared
to the invention of light itself!

It's you who decides

on your mission and fate.

How else could you learn

of your gift to create?

CHAPTER

4

Well, by now it should be obvious that these Adventurers weren't your normal, everyday kind of Adventurers. They were creative Adventurers on a mission—to have as much fun as could possibly be imagined—and to that end, as you well know, they've been wildly successful, though they have met-up with a few wrinkles that are *still* being ironed out.

For instance, once TIME was invented, the Adventurers spent so much of it playing as a creation amongst their own creations that they began to lose *themselves*. For example, during their unending games

of hide-and-seek, they stayed
HUMAN for so long, not wanting to
be found of course, that they actually
began to forget they were also
"everywhere else" at once.

And as if all that wasn't unfortunate
enough, they began bumping into one
another's thoughts and creations, adding

their own energy to each. And by then,
with so many thoughts and things and
HUMANS roaming about, it had become
difficult telling one apart from the other,
or remembering who created what. All in
all, their existence had become very
unpredictable, with the welcome exceptions
of certain recurring objects and events —
those that had simply received more
attention (more thoughts) than the others
had. Not realizing this, however, they
embraced these things for their
dependability. These, they thought, must
prove that some Realities, whether of
thoughts or things, are Expressed

by All Life.

Henceforth,

these they labeled,

with great relief, REAL.

Silly Adventurers!

Silly because they promptly set off

labeling everything they ever knew as either

real or unreal, warning each other not to

trust the unreal, lest they be made a fool of.

Oooh!

REALITIES ARE EXPRESSED BY ALL LIFE

REAL

BY ALL LIFE

37

BECOMES ★ EXAMPLES OF ★
★ BELIEF
A LIVING IDEA ★ EMBRACED AS FACT

M

Believe in yourself
and soon you will see,
how happy and free
you were meant to be.

CHAPTER

5

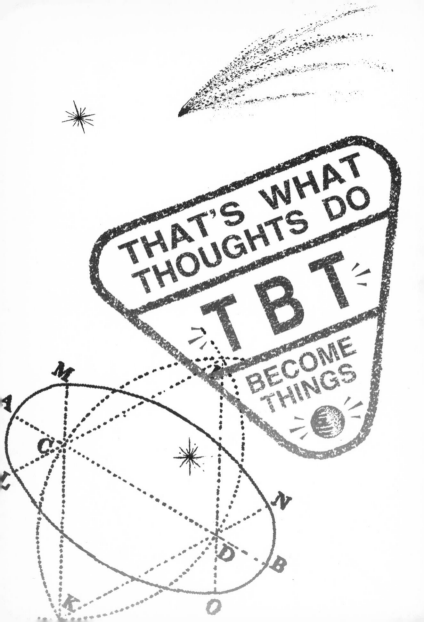

Actually, without knowing any better, they had begun assembling the very first BELIEF systems (some of which remains within the very same SPACE that you now reside!). And all because a few teeny, tiny, recurring thoughts had Become Examples of a Living Idea (because all thought is energy, or alive) Embraced as Fact. Completely forgetting a cardinal rule of creation: "To think is to limit." Not that there's anything wrong with thinking, my

gosh, but one ought to
remember that all thoughts
are just decisions, decisions that can be
changed, and with such changes new worlds
are born.

You see, no thought or idea is more
"right," or real, than another. Thoughts
are just thoughts. But when one thought

is thought enough, to the exclusion of
others even, it begins to take on a

A LIVING IDEA * BECOMES * EXAMPLES OF * BELIEF EMBRACED AS FACT

consistency,

momentum, and

reality all its own. Which, again,

is fine and all, because that's

what thoughts do... become things.

The challenge, however, is remembering

that there are always other perspectives, or

thoughts, than the ones you've chosen to

experience... blah, blah, blah. Anyway, as

TIME marched on, with their "facts," or

BELIEFS, in tow, instead of "just being

HUMAN," most began *thinking* of

themselves as "just HUMAN beings."

Hypnotized by their BELIEFS and

confounded by their illusions, the

43

Adventurers fell into a deeper and deeper trance. In fact, so far did they fall, that they began to feel trapped within their bodies and helpless among their creations. No longer did they notice that they themselves were the ones crafting the objects and events of their lives with their thoughts; instead they saw these "things" as something to contend with.

Dun, dun, dun, du-u-u-u-u-n!

They became so enraptured with what they were doing that most had even forgotten they were

really one Great Omniscient Deity.
Some were even beginning to Deny their
earlier Understandings of how Matter
Began, just asking for trouble, and were
starting to look pretty, well... we'll let
you finish the sentence.

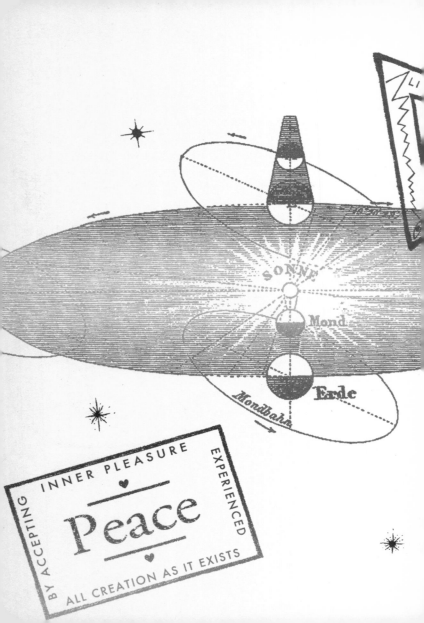

SONNE

Mond

Erde

Mondbahn

INNER PLEASURE

EXPERIENCED

BY ACCEPTING

Peace

ALL CREATION AS IT EXISTS

Blessed are emotions,

for though some make you weep,

you're better to have known them

for the secrets that they keep.

Nord Pol

CHAPTER

6

$\textrm{A}$ direct result

of their new naiveté

led to their first taste of FEAR, which was

felt whenever they Failed to Experience the

Actual Reality before them. A scary thing

they soon found out. No fun at all! And

worse, a whole hoard of emotions sprang to

life with their every misunderstanding.

At first they appeared slowly, each

felt to the extent a truth, any truth, was

being misunderstood; but because so much

more was being understood so much less,

they started experiencing their emotions

so much faster!

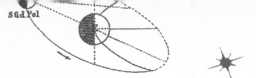

As we watched what was happening we
were devastated. Never, in any reality, had
such lofty Beings plunged into such great
despair. Terror, sadness, anger, and guilt
were rampant. It was almost too much for
us to bear, not to mention what they put
themselves through, poor "things"! It was a
travesty through and through until, little by
little, there began a great healing—not from
on-high or any other such "place" (though
some still say it was a Mystically
Incited Reality Adjustment
Concealed by Loving Entities);
it was a healing we now
understand that had transpired

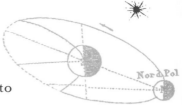

from within.

Life ministering to

life itself—perhaps a MIRACLE either way.

It turns out that the Adventurers were

learning from their emotions, and as they

did, so did we. For example, if FEAR stems

from the Failure to Experience the Actual

Reality before you, then at least it serves as

an unmistakable warning (to the one doing

the "fearing"), that his or her *thinking*

has strayed from the truth. And though

it may seem for some that the warning

appears too late, it actually emerges in its

exaggerated state only after other emotions

served similar notice, but were ignored.

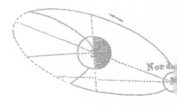

There was even more good news about these emotions. It turned out they could be warm and fuzzy too, or happy and silly. Some were even wild and crazy! And it was their passage through all the emotions, happy and sad, they told us later, that brought the "Illustrious Ones" (as they came to be called) their greatest achievement: an inner Pleasure Experienced by Accepting all Creation as it Exists, or inner PEACE.

Mastered by so few because it requires a *deep* understanding of the perfection that exists within everything, every moment, every place, and everyone, *no matter what*!

WHY YOU DO

LIFE AFTER LIFE?

WHAT YOU DO

Life's an illusion

just waiting for you…

to act on your dreams

so that they can come true.

CHAPTER

7

THE SPIRIT OF LIFE

SET FREE

OF

SET FREE

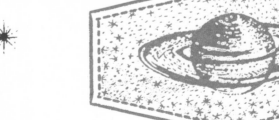

Strange as this may sound, as life revealed unto life and we watched the Adventurers with their learning, we noticed something that most there have not yet seen for themselves: that as they believe, they become, and somewhere in-between believing and becoming, without fail, they ACT.

You see, if they hold a thought long enough, they begin to move with it, and this movement itself actually hastens the manifestation process profoundly because it emboldens their belief that success will be achieved—ultimately

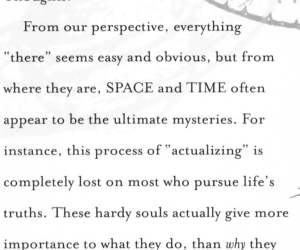

Actualizing, into
Concrete terms, their
Thoughts!

From our perspective, everything "there" seems easy and obvious, but from where they are, SPACE and TIME often appear to be the ultimate mysteries. For instance, this process of "actualizing" is completely lost on most who pursue life's truths. These hardy souls actually give more importance to what they do, than *why* they do what they do—life after life after life.

Some meditate quietly on cliffs, as if they could get any closer to the angels that already rest upon their shoulders. Others think the path to understanding might be found by escaping who they think they are, as if the answers they seek could be found by hiding from their questions. And then there are those who belittle, criticize, and nit-pick themselves to pieces... as if concentrating on what's wrong will suddenly reveal all that's right.

There's more, too. There are those who feel they should read the right stuff, talk the right stuff, eat the right stuff, or go to the right places, at the right times, with the right people... as if they thought "somebody" else was actually keeping track... and grading them!

The only actions that matter, we've seen, are those that follow beliefs, but then that's true of all actions, so the point worth noting here is that due to the "simultaneosity" of it all (shhhhh...)

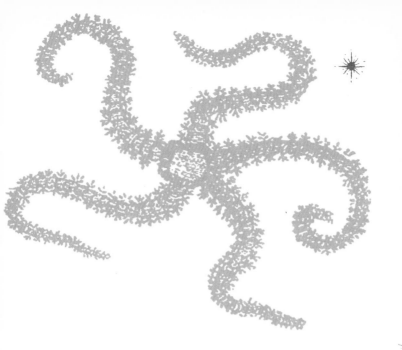

the reverse is also true. By taking action

towards a desired result, the belief that the

result will soon manifest is intensified,

accelerating its entry into space and time!

In the depths of space,

there isn't a trace,

of the power that brought it to be.

But if you look inside,

it cannot hide,

it was the Spirit of Life set free.

CHAPTER

8

By now, all forms of awareness, from everywhere ever thought of, have heard about space, time, and the brilliant Adventurers who created it all. And those who drop by for a look are so astounded by what they find in this little corner of creation that they're changed forever.

It's not just the splendor of the planets, or the raging life that thrives upon them, or even the bold, outrageous thoughts that continue to perpetuate it all. Observers are left speechless and are downright humbled by the few who have returned from the adventure—those Adventurers who have actually found *themselves* amidst the games and learning, and in doing so have become far more than the sum of their experience, more than who they thought they were when it all began.

These are the "Illustrious Ones," whose glowing radiance and divine illumination reflect an understanding rooted in the unshakable knowledge that all things and events are born of thought (their own), that in space and time it's all good (if you believe in bad), and that everything, everywhere, is *always* God.

Only by losing themselves and serving their

illusions, could these Adventurers then be driven emotionally — by their burning desires—to reclaim and know the depths of their own divinity. And by deeply *understanding* that their very own thoughts, words and actions, alone, determine what's "meant to be," they've reached such a state of supreme bliss and all-knowingness that they've become the inspiration and the ideal that all who have met them strive for.

Now, having just shared this, it is a bit amazing to us—not a problem mind you, just amazing—that more have not joined the ranks of the Illustrious Ones.

Certainly to each his (or her) own;
it's just that they're all still so
caught up in this most awesome
adventure of theirs, it seems they
really couldn't care less about
"everywhere else"!

Perhaps you understand them better.
Still, to us at least, it seems a shame that
such inexhaustible energy and creative
genius is being so thoroughly neglected. If
they could—and we assure you, they can—
just for an instant, glimpse their greater
reality and see themselves as the
omniscient, unlimited, fun-loving

gladiators they've always been, it would so radically change everything. Not that they should "return." Heavens, no! We just think that they might have a better... "TIME," shall we say, if reminded that they, themselves, are God. Don't you think?

Anyway, enough of all that. The real reason we wrote this little book was to get your attention, and let you know... *we've blown the lid clear-off your little charade—HA*! FOUND YOU!

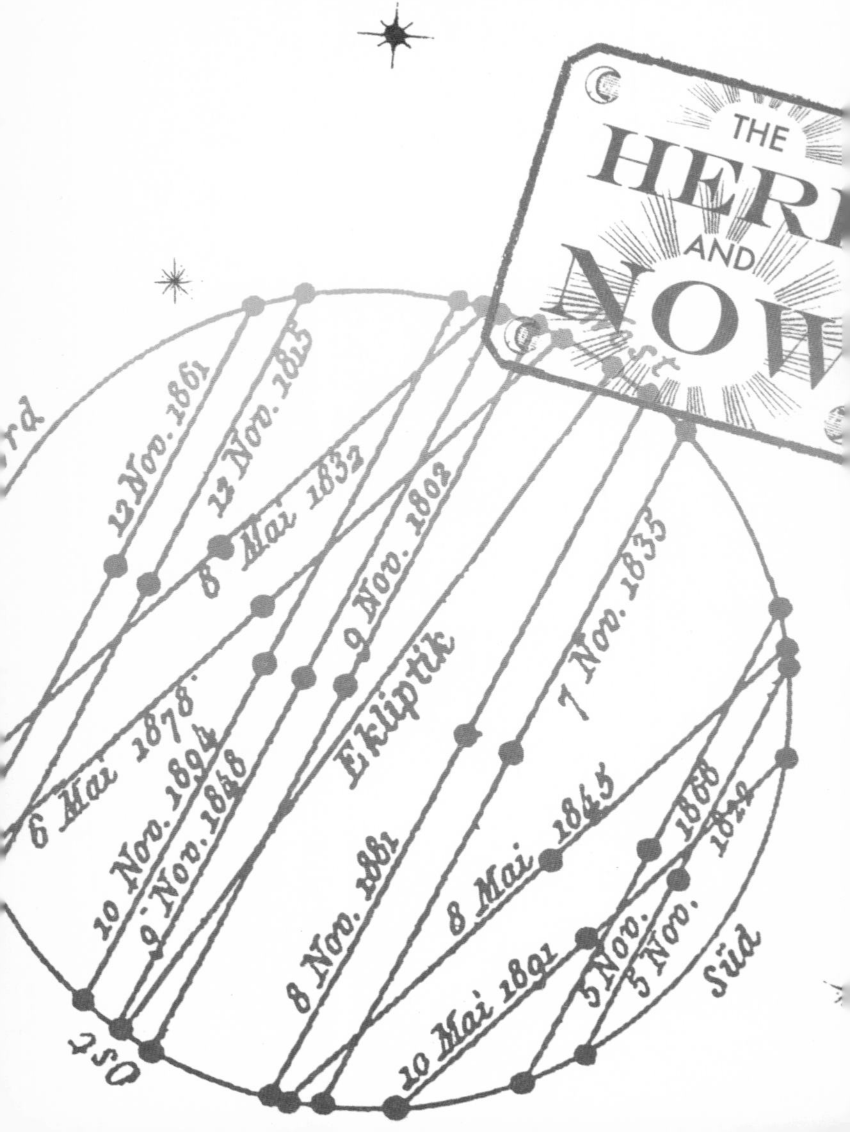

THE
HER[
AND
NOW

6 Mai 1878
12 Nov. 1861
13 Nov. 1815
8 Mai 1832
9 Nov. 1802
7 Nov. 1835
10 Nov. 1894
9 Nov. 1848
Ekliptik
8 Nov. 1861
8 Mai 1845
1868
1822
10 Mai 1891
5 Nov.
5 Nov. 1899
Ost
Süd

Well?

... you're still reading... not a good...

C'mon Love, snap to it! Stop kidding

around... There's literally a trillion

things...

Yes YOU! Of course YOU! Who else is

reading this *here and now*?

Arghhh... another one lost... in SPACE.

Epilogue —

The Meaning of Life

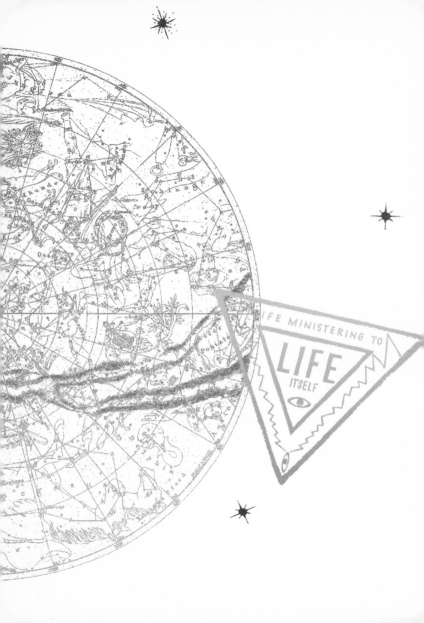

Okay, okay, that wasn't so fair. We knew all along that you were lost.

Actually, we know a lot more about you than you might think.

Listen up, old friend (older than you can even fathom): You were the brave one among us—so brave in fact that you kind of left us in your dust. You see, none of us have even tried SPACE and TIME yet, because we wanted to see how you turned out!

Really, you haven't been gone for as long as we like to joke, but before you left we agreed to be your lifeline, your angels,

just in case you ever called. We've done
our part, all right, and have been there
each and every time you so much as said,
"Ouch!" (though we did pitch the white
winged costumes you made us wear for your
"Going Somewhere" party). Our point is
this: You've done such a bang-up job, we're
all more than a little anxious to
get going with our turns, though
we're afraid you'll be angry if
we abandon our posts.

We've rationalized a bit
and figure that at your
rate of progress, you don't
really need us anymore. Besides, as

it turns

out, there's

very little we can

actually do for you here other than rant

and rave from the "bleachers." You

wouldn't have it any other way, remember?

You understand, don't you?

What's more (and we didn't know this

when you left), once we begin our own

adventures, we'll remain in touch and

within reach, available at your slightest call,

though consciously none of us will likely

know just what's going on.

Anyway, we made our decision some

time ago, before you even began this

lifetime, and have each planned
our way into the very same SPACE and
TIME where you now reside. In fact, one
of us just might be that loud neighbor
of yours... Aha! And in case you were
beginning to wonder, we also arranged
for your finding this little book through
the "simultaneosity" we spoke of earlier
(we snuck into the future). You don't still
believe in coincidence, do you?

So that you don't feel too put out, we

smuggled in the following excerpt from
one of the Illustrious One's latest
memoirs, to hopefully tip the
scales in your quest for

78

understanding. Adios amigo, and until we meet again, remember:

Life is not about hiding and seeking, nor is it about learning the things you've forgotten; it's not even about remembering them. It's about BEING—BEING YOURSELF! You were Born to Expand the Infinite Nature of God.

Live only to be who you now are. You are Creation's first and last hope to fill the shoes you alone can fashion, and eternity will pass before this chance will come again. You are the dream of a legion before you who have passed on the torch of time and space awareness so that your mere existence could immeasurably enrich all that is: God. By simply BEING, you will fulfill this dream, centered in the

here and now, where all dreams

come true, all truths reside, and

understanding is born.

Your sacred heart was hewn at the dawn

of creation in a dance to celebrate the birth of

forever; you can do no wrong. There are no "shoulds"

or "shouldn'ts" and no "rights" or "wrongs." Life is

not about being happy or sad, good or bad. It's not even

about making your dreams come true; that much

is inevitable.

There is only BEING. Eternal BEING.

 Inescapable BEING. You are perfect; it is done.

Your rare and precious light has, and will forevermore,

illuminate the worlds you create—the worlds that

now wait for your blessed BEING.

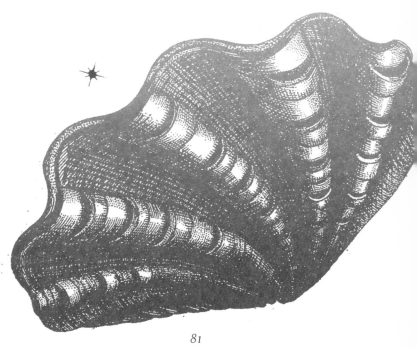

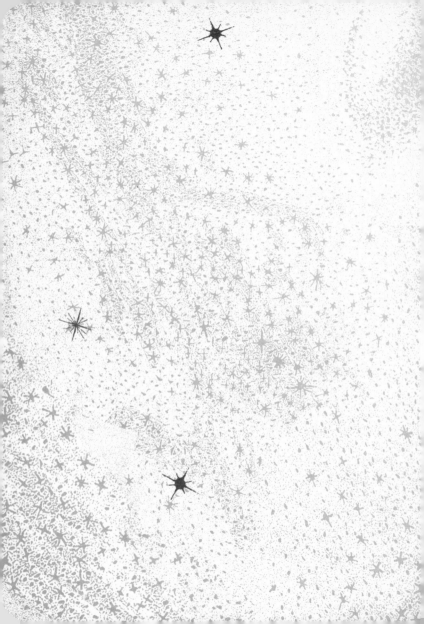

P.S.

We love you.

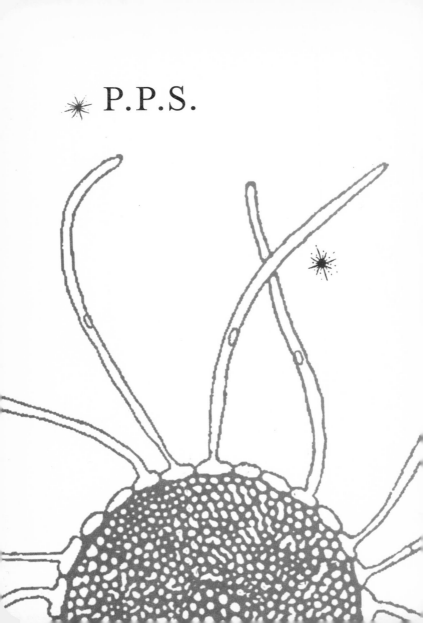

P.P.S.

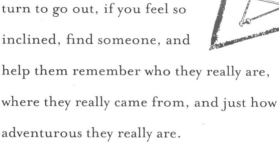

So... you know what all this means, don't you? It means you're "it"! Now it's your turn to go out, if you feel so inclined, find someone, and help them remember who they really are, where they really came from, and just how adventurous they really are.

But before you go, here are some final thoughts that may help you, as well as those you find, to begin having an even better time, here and now:

The Seven Spiritual Laws of Thriving in Time and Space

1. You are now who and where you most wanted to be— go with it.

2. Where you are is never who you are —you're always more.

3. Thoughts become things — choose them wisely, dream big, visualize.

4. When you want change, physically do something about it, every single day.

5. You're never alone; friends abound whether you can see them or not.

6. Everything is as it should be; there've been no mistakes.

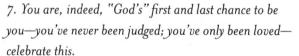

7. You are, indeed, "God's" first and last chance to be you—you've never been judged; you've only been loved— celebrate this.

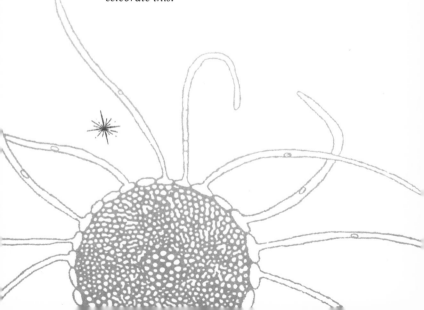

Fellow Adventurer, your time in space is a priceless treasure that will never come again. And though you'll live forever, the opportunities you now have, some of which are disguised as challenges, are irreplaceable, and among these are your precious dreams. You were among the illustrious architects who dreamed up this bastion of perfection in the cosmos and now you are the very reason the sun rises each morning. Understand, then, to the core of your being, that you're already worthy and deserving of anything else your heart may desire in this dream within a dream. Ain't life grand?

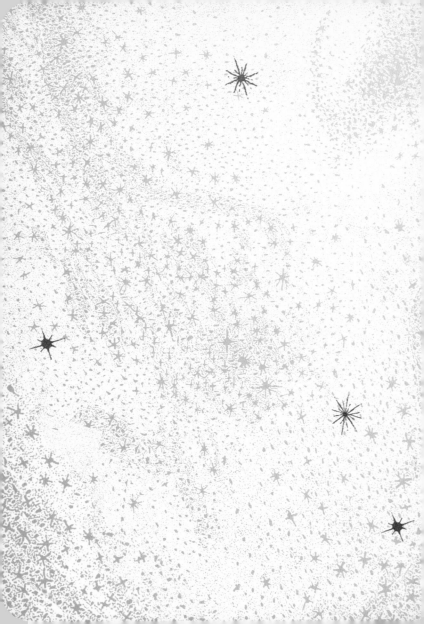

Revelations,

Epiphanies and Discoveries

Video Message!